Best Time Spent

Love and BTS - A Poetic Journey

-Neha Bhardwaj Tiwari

Title: Best Time Spent
Subtitle: Love and BTS – A Poetic Journey
Author: Neha Bhardwaj Tiwari
ISBN (Paperback): 978-93-342-5837-0

Self Published By: Neha Bhardwaj Tiwari

Printed and distributed by: (In India)
Mudranik Technologies Pvt. Ltd. Ground Floor, No. 46, 11th cross, Indiranagar, 1st stage, Bengaluru 560038, Karnataka.

Printed and distributed by: (Outside India)
Amazon KDP

For more information email:
neha.bhardwaj7520@gmail.com

Dedication

Dedicated to you my reader family
To one of the largest fandoms, to ARMY.
Dedicated to ones who paved the way,
The BTS boys who have slayed!

About the Author

Neha's love for writing started even before Orkut was a thing. (Orkut was basically Facebook before Facebook took over) But passion took a backseat to practicality. She spent years navigating the corporate world, climbing ladders, and checking all the "right" boxes—until life threw her a plot twist.

During the covid lockdown, while on sabbatical from work and embracing motherhood, she rediscovered her long-lost dream of writing. Turns out, sleep deprivation and endless baby bottles can also spark creativity!

When she's not weaving stories, Neha enjoys swimming, cycling, and chess—at least, that's what she tells people. Her real hobbies? binge-watching Netflix, indulging in retail therapy, and fangirling over BTS.

She lives in Mumbai, India, with her family.

Connect:
Instagram: @neha.bhardwaj.14268
Facebook: neha.bhardwaj.14268
Kakao Talk: someday

****

Introduction

"Love does not claim possession but gives freedom."
- Rabindranath Tagore

Falling in love has a way of turning us into poets, and for ARMY, love for BTS is no exception. This collection is more than just poetry—it's a heartfelt, nostalgic journey through emotions, imaginations and the magic of Bangtan.

Whether you're a casual listener or an adorable representative MC for youth, get ready to challenge yourself and test your knowledge on RM, Jin, Suga, J-Hope, Jimin, V & JK and have fun along the way.

This book speaks to those who want to visit Hybe and are captivated with BTS's music, concerts and Weverse lives. Seen through the eyes of a devoted fan, these verses offer a glimpse into Bangtan's world—one where music heals, dreams take flight and love knows no limits.

As you turn these pages, may you relive your memories and just like with their music, may reading this book be your best time spent too.

****

Table of Contents

Before reading, please do the fan chant

Kim Namjoon
Kim Seokjin
Min Yoongi
Jung Hoseok
Park Jimin
Kim Taehyung
Jeon Jungkook

BTS

The Leader

Real
Marvellous

Brainy and brawny
charismatic and simple,
a gorgeous guy
a book lover with a dimple.

Indigo sky, winter flower
all remind of you,
lost in Seoul town road
with a bicycle to the rescue.
Break the code:
I don't need a boyfriend
I have you.

Look here in my heart
seven right people at the right place,
you're not just a green flag
but a whole green forest
giving me solace.

Go around the world in a day
but come back closer to me,
"Life is soup & I'm a fork",
your words are my therapy…

Never out of love
never lonely,
as I have your
treasured (rkived) memories.

Nicest of the nicest being
also, a public relations ambassador for
ministry of national defence,
Just manifesting happiness
on a random day
or on a special one
nestled with your presence.

****

The Worldwide Handsome One

Jewel
In
Nature

Mirrors are few, don't take two
on another level
see your reflection in my eyes
don't need a friend, I have you.

A killer rapper intoxicating with IGIN,
nothing without your love
but this gaming lover Gucci boy
in love with super tuna's fin.

Queens queueing up to meet his eyes
a heart in a window,
a mellifluous singer living life 'king size'.
Mild or spicy version? a difficult choice
flavor not version, Jin ramen is my appetite.

Please say you love me
scattered thoughts; running wild
fancy like a silver spoon
is one handsome face worldwide…

Wrapped around his wide shoulders
wish it was only me
alas! it’s one lucky alpaca plushie

"I'm the one I should love"
“I will come to you” a voice echoes
in love with this person, oh so mushy.

Beyond my reach is my happy place
yet I'll be there in the background
like an astronaut in outer space,
as once in a blue moon
might be able to see his pretty face.

Somewhere, sometime
evenings with ‘Eat Jin’
or listening to abyss,
keen on being ‘the one’
Just a wish,
immersed wholly
near your worldwide beautiful bliss.

****

The Savage One

Seductive
Unique
Good-looking
Alluring

A skilled dancer
a fast-paced rapper
savage but sweet
just like sugar.

What do you think
am I the girl of your dreams?
when will D day come?
when the Daegu town king
meets his queen.

Valentino, NBA all want you
the queue is never ending
ARMY's proposals aren't few.
Decipher the cypher, why so serious?
“I don't need a husband"
I have you.

Fortunate is piano
and the strings of guitar,
beautiful fingers play on it
"Daechwita, Suchwita"...

Listen boy, my first love story
hot as one can be
loyal as one can be
no wonder all the girls say, including me:
"Yoongi marry me."

You know I love you
on days I'm cheerful
on days I'm laden with woes,
never felt this close
getting together or not
I won't stop to propose.

****

The Dance Leader

Joyful
Handsome
Optimistic
Pure
Euphoric

Music to my ears
and a breath of fresh air,
the sunshine of the group
a dance machine with flair.

A precious jewel
a buttercup flower
LV is okay
he himself is a super power.

Rap songs to look forward for
hot hip thrusts to die for,
my 'important business' can wait
it's you who I live for.

Be it a mad rush hour
judging is your arson,
no more blue side
the thunderous laughter
spreads joy to each person…

A live wire, but
chicken noodle soup calms you down,
I wonder in my sweet dreams
a smile on my face when you're around.

A warrior on the streets of Gwangju
unlock the lock:
not just a hope size teddy
need a diamond necklace too.

Uplifted ~~SPRITE~~ spirit and saved from downslope
hope you find your Mona Lisa,
For me you are my world, my hope.

Hope is synonymous with him
obvious it is,
Someone so special
endearing it is.
overwhelmed with love, a definite
keeper he is.

****

Sexy, Cutie, Lovely

Passionate
And
Real
Kind

A popstar, an idol, a heartthrob
he is every girl's dream come true.
Ah! excuse me
I am in that queue too.

His hair flips make me smile
his smile makes me drool,
sexy, cutie, lovely
he is a singer who is super cool.

Full of love are his lyrics
melting my heart with bliss.
A man who's a true blue
he's a song writer too.

His sultry moves
gets me wooed,
how not to fall for him
he's a dancer too…

A boy from Bangtan
who's ruling my heart; I never knew
how much I love him
he has no clue!

Just waiting forever
imagining things unreal,
Most of the time
inadvertently
never felt more real.

****

The Good Boy

Versatile, Victorious

Branded from head to toe
a compose coffee lover,
manly and strong
yet inner child young forever.

Wild like a winter bear
soft like a snow flower,
in a life of blue & grey
purple ocean is my power.

A deep voice
hypnotizing again,
a sweet night
when you love me again.

The most handsome man
for over a decade,
a horseback rider, a saxophone player
a singer with songs to serenade.

Don't need an oppa, I have you,
cold winter's scenery
under a Christmas tree
can I layover on you?...

Wherever you are in this microcosmos
for us,
can we be friends?
as even if I die its only you.

Together better
always in a dreamlike place,
every time I imagine
hollowness fades.
Your singularity is
unique,
navigating love
gearing up getting intrigued.

****

Golden Maknae

Jewelled
King

Tattooed arms
mafia vibes
a kid at heart with doe eyes,
fuelling my delusions
with flirtatious Weverse lives.

A golden boy like a tiger lily
standing next to me physically...?
shot glass filled with tears of joy
if closer to me in 3D.

Don't need a friend I have you
thank you
for keeping that dreamer in me alive,
still with you
no matter who comes left & right.
Am I too sad to dance? never,
my you, you who are bright.

Michael told me in the closet
this somebody is vivacious,
please don't change
all seven of you are precious...

Nobody can hate you
you have that euphoria,
yes or no? no one can deny the fact
BTS is the heart of Korea.

Jack of all trades, master of everything
unwavering love
never let go
gorgeousness mounting.
Killing with his aura
on the go,
on top of the world
knowing him is love for sure.

****

Guess the Title

Can't fight this war of hormone
your dimple makes me go, go in paradise.
Drop your mic for you I will croon
I love you, my Kim Namjoon.

In unfamiliar streets of Korea, I roam
fly me in an airplane to your home.
Let's eat ramen with a silver spoon
'Coz, I love you so much my Jin moon.

Everyone likes to propose to you
but you run away like fire,
hold me tight, my love is not over
I love you so much my Min Suga.

To dance with you give me permission
it won't be a bad decision,
your presence is dynamite, it is dope
I love you so much my J Hope.

I know we are bulletproof
but your love has pierced my soul,
Keep no filter and open up your heart to me
I love you so much my Jiminshi...

Don't think my love is savage
forever it is meant to be,
in rainy days, slow dance with me
love you so much, my Taehyung, my V.

I'm fine but not young forever
but I'll always be your girl with love,
Busan I'm yet to come someday
I'll love you always my JK.

Life goes on, but don't leave me, not today
I'm a butterfly in danger with tear.
Save me my black swan,
make it right, my Bangtan Sonyeondan.

****

Guess the Title part 2

You made me love myself and have no fear
the film is out,
forever indebted
swear on my blood, sweat & tears.

Earlier I had no more dreams
now I jump with euphoria.
Be it autumn, winter or spring day
24/7 your love runs in my DNA.

Hold me tight my friend
hug me right till the end,
all my sorrows gone with your caress
love you my BTS.

You're so far, yet so near
every time I miss you
in my dreams you appear.
With ARMYs shield
no one can attack on Bangtan
born singer, love you Bangtan.

My idol, my universe, my man,
save me, come to ma city
I need you my Anpanman...

Thank you for coming in my life
you gave me wings to fly.
Be it zero O clock of any day
hope I meet you just one day.

Don't ask me proof
my dreams are dark & wild.
Give me a map of Seoul,
so, I'll never walk alone.

If you're cold, I'll be your fire
if you're hungry, I'll be your butter
but never think this is fake love
'Coz I will love nobody other.

The most beautiful moment in life
is the rise of Bangtan,
in love with a boy
who is the first from Busan.

****

Best Time Spent

The 21st century girls
in love with seven normal boys of Korea,
not first love but an everlasting one
heart filled with utopia.

Same continent but a different country
wish you knew my feelings with telepathy.
A paradise of crystal snow
stay gold, I love you, you know
even though everybody said no.

The essence of my life is your presence
what am I doing now
do you think it makes sense?

Am I wrong falling in love with you?
Not miss right but there's no moving on,
awake not lost
still with you, now and beyond.

Snow feels loved with your touch
rain feels special drizzling on you,
invisible but essential
let me be the air around you…

Two sides of the same coin
friends or soulmates?
dreamers of an unknown fate,
today and tomorrow
not just coffee but want a ramyeon date.

Because togethers special
Because tomorrows surreal.
Present is heaven with purple hues
Best time spent is thinking about you.

****

When

When Gangnam style was the only one
and Hangul was never heard of,
when Seoul was just a city
and Busan, Daegu were never heard of.

When Korea was just another country
and K-pop / K-drama were never heard of,
when subtitles became a way of life
K-wave swooped in our hearts.

When Samantha & Rachel were just names
and Rebecca wasn't a car,
when K meant Kite or Kangaroo
and K-world was afar.

When "you want to eat ramen?" was innocent
and noodles were all in the mind,
when 7 was just any number
the most innocent fandom helped unwind.

When purple meant love
and love language was finger hearts,
when seven kings ruled the kingdom
they paved the way with their craft!

****

Double Nonet

I
was just
ordinary.
You made me feel
loved, wanted, special.
You gave me hope to live.
I was just lost in my thoughts
in myself, you made me believe.
Relieved, you brought the best out of me.

Not scared of falling down I'm upbeat.
At crossroads of life, you helped me
What matters is inner peace.
No looking back from here,
I'll keep my promise
I am yours dear.
You found me
I am
here.

****

A Date

Dear diary,
far away in the land of Korea
a lovely boy stealing a million hearts,
can't fathom my love for him
near me yet miles apart.

He doesn't know I exist
his endearing aura I can't resist.
He's the brightest star
I am mere blade of grass.
A distant dream far away from reality
my happiness is living in this duality.

On an island named Jeju
drinking wine and some soju,
sweeter than mochi
tastier than carbonara,
a date with someone who calls it lachimolala.

A Libran boy
as sensuous as the moon in the blue sky,
13 is a lucky number
on the date of October 1995...

In this lifetime or next
will I ever be seeing
he who is
jovial, intelligent, melodious, incredibly nice
being...?

****

Run with BTS

It's okay to not be okay and yearn
wish I was 18 again or 25, 21,
would've fought for my way
been happy and on the run.
A queen of smiles and not tears
a lovely runner without any fears.

An extraordinary attorney, a modern farmer
a taxi driver or just a strong girl named Boon,
business proposals coming my way
me, chilling with squid games till noon.

Oh, descendants of the sun
bless me with a golden spoon,
can't do a money heist
crash land me in Bangtan's room.

Always Bangtan boys over flowers
and ugh! not some random love next door,
Oh legend of the blue sea
bring me to the Korean shores.

When life gives you tangerines
need vacations in Waikiki
and a sky castle in Seoul,
I'll be in a train to Busan
please let him love me more…

A celebrity, a true beauty
BTS is legendary.
Wish I am destined with them
before all of us are dead,
are you sure?
yes, that's all in my heart & my head.

****

Dream

Woken up in my youth with a dreamy glow
a night in a strange city
a brand-new day in Seoul.

Too cool for school
seven normal boys in their teens
teleported in a jiffy to the year 2013.

If time travel is what it takes
I'll do it in a heartbeat,
would you turn off your phone
and look here pleased?

Don't ask me where did I come from
I'll let you know when it's time to wake up
134340 your number I'll save up.

I'll hold onto it in 'my time'
a girl in love needs some more dream,
don't ask me to rise and shine.

What if the pandora's box is open
and there's nothing more to stop it?
daydreaming a hope of safety zone aligns
need a piece of peace with equal sign…

Happiness is:
Seven kings of the purple kingdom
and living with them like royalty

Dream disappearing like a house of cards,
in a click of the light stick
moved on to reality.

****

Love

As the night enfolds
imagining being with you,
smiling ear to ear
blushing when near you.

Eyes transfixed on my honey
stargazing my moon,
on a secluded island
sitting beside a bon-fire
heartbeat skipping a tune.

Wind gushing through hair
water brushing our feet,
from dawn to dusk
holding hands till shadows meet.

A question in my mind
how are you so fine,
want you to want me
for just the way I am.

You are at a place; no one can replace
need you to need me,
my heart is aligned
three & half hours ahead in time…

Two parallel lines that never meet
feet back on reality,
a different kind of mutual love
a fan and a celebrity?

What is love
honesty, care, romance?
love is unconditional
just need a chance.
As in some theories
parallel lines do meet in a trance.

You are love, love is you
don't need or want anything,
you are with me
and I am with you.

****

Bittersweet

Forgotten how it felt to be loved
forgotten how it felt to have butterflies,
forgotten to be swept off my feet
remembering what each day looks like.

Forgotten to be cared for
forgotten to be someone's priority,
forgotten to be pampered
remembering the disparities.

No more expectations
beyond the repair stage,
time can't heal those wounds
as fresh cuts appear on the way.

Don't need the appreciation
don't need the acknowledgement
don't need anybody else,
a reminder to always 'Love Yourself'.

Comfort in these pure words
the message touched a million hearts,
it wiped my tears
made me realize what I'm worthy of…

Got back the butterflies
got back the blush
got back the smile
got the reason to trust.

Found a new strength
found a new love,
wounds healed
its traces blurred.

Out of my league
will never possibly meet
still a hope to live by every single day,
will live a lifetime
even if it’s a second's stay.

An impossible dream yet I run
no matter I become an old woman,
love's an intrinsic nature
after all, I am just human.

****

Reverie

Too forlorn on the nights alone
lost in reverie
into your eyes I've drowned.

Dreams keeping me alarmed
do your thing with me now.
Fly to my room with that gaze
with your love maze
I have been swarmed.

Spine breaker moves
but stay closer than this,
louder than bombs are the sounds
for I have been crowned.

Hold me like there's no tomorrow
your eyes tell, love has no bounds
the magic shop is open
can we go around?

Sweet as sugar, salty like butter
somebody like a fine wine,
cross the baseline, it's definitely you
a dreamy Tony Montana could be mine?...

Out of reverie, out of misery
experienced an epiphany,
all that I need is
some 'champagne & confetti'.

****

In a World

In a world of flaunting
some people are modest,
in a world of swindlers
some people are honest.

In a world of filters
best things are natural,
in a world of delusions
many things are factual.

In a world of short attention span
K-dramas are binge watched,
in a world of global music
few songs are etched in our hearts.

In a world of sadness
a silver lining incorporates,
in a world of fast paced life
'Love Myself' a message resonates.

In a world of darkness
sun shines on the other side,
in a world of constant judging
made peace with the inner side…

In a world of changes
somethings are always constant,
in a world of betrayal
ARMYs are loyal and ardent.

In a world of DM
love letters are a scarcity,
in a world of breakups
true love is a rarity.

In a world of AI
things are surreal,
in a world of fake love
somethings are real.

Reality hurts
in a world of fibs,
but in a world of hope,
hope still exists.

****

Song

Sing this to the tune of 'Bad Decisions'...

Seoul subway station G E T, L single O Ve

It's not a secret, I love you ssshh,
you're light of my life, I swear I can't resist.
I want your love, don't need your fame
tell me do you also feel the same?

If you love me back
show me some gesture
don't make me say.

Please give some, love expressions
I want you, ooh baby, to be mine.

So just leave, all your 'Mrs.'...
I want you every year, month, week, day & night
and it'll be like, ooh, ah
I'll be never ever out of your sight
and it'll be like, ooh, ah,
I want you, ooh baby, to be mine…

Everybody envious and cries (oh, yeah)
and the reason's obvious there's no surprise (oh, yeah)
'Coz we're together side by side (oh, yeah)
and I can't imagine you faraway
would never let you go astray.

If you love me back
show me some gesture
don't make me say.

I won't jump, to any conclusions
you're welcome to say no anytime,
hey it's your life and your say
I'm content in one sided love anyway.
Its unfathomable, it's not understood
but it always feels right, it feels good.

Let's make some right decisions
you in me and I in you (dancing)
will you give the permission?

****

You

BTS POV:

A regional idol
you made us global,
a singer, a dancer, a rapper
you put us on a pedestal.
You said we paved the way,
you were with us in our struggles.
We were locals, you made us global.

We will strive hard for you
your admiration gives us strength,
we'll continue making our music
your support takes us to great lengths.

Let us hear your story
you know a lot about us,
let no one hurt you
trust yourself first.
Wish we could meet you all but it's tough
this one lifetime isn't enough.

In 10, 20 years down the line
you may forget us and move on,
but we will remember you always
our fans who carried us on…

Feels good to be loved
let us reciprocate it to you
you are mine,
ARMY, you are our family too.

Come what may
we know you will support us
we really mean it when we say,
you are my universe.

****

ARMY

ARMY POV:

Ayo ladies & gentleman
our superhero, our new generation Anpanman
we love this singer, this man.

You sing: "save me, save me
I need your love before I fall"
as if you are reading our mind
“Fire, Fire” our distress call.

On a single toe or a single foot, we'll jump
when we hear you say:
" I need you girl " or
“Run beautiful, run, yeah, you got to run”.

Say what you want, say what you want
we believe everything you sing, like:
"You're my best friend for the rest of my life or
"Tell me what you want right now, hello,
I'ma give it to you girl right now".

Don't ever think we'll forget you, not me
Oh are you crazy, you,
You must be kidding me
don't believe me?...

just say: "so show me", I'll show you
"so, show me", I'll prove it to you.

That dimple is illegal but we want it anyway
can't close our eyes, you're taking over us tonight.
Let's make some bad decisions tonight
'Coz when we fall, we know how to land
'Coz we, we are in the stars tonight.

Oh my, my, my, smooth like butter
we flirt with the boys we love
you know it all, love it's so mad
you're our best friend, love you so bad.

See me, see me, yeah; not a liar
we wanna be good,
just for you
we wanna be strong,
just for you
you have us, we have you
we are forever bulletproof.

We call you artist; we call you idol
we call you much more in fan fictions & Wattpad,
'Coz your love we miss that
your love we want that
your touch we need that...

My everything, my blood, sweat & tears
got no fears, we're singing:
the best moment is yet to come,
when we bump into each other
and together run, run, run.

And you gonna be happy
we'll keep on running & running until we catchup,
where the party yeah
hope this airplane we don’t miss up.

Millions of us and you're only seven
but that is okay,
hope you find a pretty woman
but just not, not today.

Future is unforeseen
but what if that moment's right now, right?
yeah, life goes on
but we know who can make it right.

****

Cinquain

Love
adorable, affectionate
admiring, respecting, caring
a feeling easy to express, just 1 word
BTS

****

Manifest

Whisper sweet nothings
take me out of Mills & Boon,
take me to the stars
seeing you I'm already on the moon.

A slight touch
raising my heartbeats,
a whiff of your presence
I'm weak on my knees.

A soft kiss
sending shivers down my spine,
your deep gaze
I'm beyond my melting point.

A light hug
shaking the floor beneath,
let it not be over
this phase of being dreamy.

Lingering on me
the presence of you
and the fragrance of your body,
too good to be true
is it a dream or delusional reality?

****

Mirrors

undeceived, real.
flattering, reminiscing, showing
reflections, emotions, nostalgia, hope.
past, present, future
believing, judging
mirror.

****

Rendezvous

A rendezvous, how will it be?
a fluttering heart when we meet,
words not coming out of my mouth
getting star-struck and having cold feet.

All choked up, hands shaking
down my cheeks tears rolling.
An introvert in a room full of K-beauty
spell-bound seeing you,
seeing you is serendipity.

Fortunate are the ones near Korean peninsula
in a blink of an eye
they can meet their oppa.
Don't know your songs, neither the lyrics correctly
all that I know is, I love you purely.

Just another fan girl at a meet & greet
rendezvous over in a jiffy,
fleeting moments cherished forever
as blissful as one can be.

A miniscule micron in your world
but you mean the whole world to me…

Hope you find the one
you've been looking for,
for me it'll always be you
I know who is my heart waiting for.

****

Tryst with Korea

Korean air calling me at Incheon airport
a spouse visa will do?
a tryst with love, I'm just going with the flow
got my documents ready as you said so.

Under the same sky
breathing the same air
landed in my fantasy land

Celebrating Chuseok
dressed up in hanbok
a tourist in Boraland.

Chimmy, Tata, Shooky, Cooky,
RJ, Koya, Mang and Van,
singing Arirang our tiny tan
that's how our BT21 universe is spanned.

In freezing winter weather
or in short sweet summers
or on a cherry blossom day
waiting to meet 'the' Hybe runner…

But sold-out tickets within minutes
what a bummer!
How to meet him
+82
just have the two digits of his number.

Hope we meet somewhere, be it gymming
or walking around arm in arm,
let the sweet sugary magic of Jin work
tryst with love is never ending...
I am serious, not just kidding.

****

More

A chance encounter
but hoping for more.

A glimpse is enough
but longing for more.

A handshake is enough
but desiring for more.

A hug is enough
but yearning for more.

A coffee is enough
but ramens galore.

A date is enough
but wanting more.

A twirl is enough
but waltzing slow.

A peck is enough
but thirsty for more…

Never met
but forever adored

A day is not enough,
night cravings are more.

****

Like

Love you
like a friend
like an idol
like a celebrity
like a star

Love you
like a crush
like a companion
like a lover
like never apart

Love you
like a boyfriend
like a husband
like soulmates
like entwined fates

Heart aches with your adoring attacks,
perks of having a long-distance relationship
it makes you a poet
who loves you to the moon & back…

Love you
like forever
like crazy
like family
like life

you're the apple of my eye
love you like this, love you like that
it's just in me, I'm naive.

****

Oppa

AMA, MAMA, Billboard, Asian artists...
numerous awards adorned,
watching on repeat
Bon voyage, Run BTS and Bangtan bombs.

Multitasking with subtitles
love, romance, K-dramas
only words learnt
annyeong, saranghae, gwenchana.

If you're the front man
or a soldier within my sight,
don't mind losing to dalgona
or red light, green light.

Kill me, heal me; oh good doctor
be my healer Mr. Sunshine,
a super(moon) in Agust or Joon
with the coffee prince of Daegu to dine.

When the phone rings I dream high
a casanova like Vincenzo
are you my destiny?
Oh my Venus, I heard your voice…

While you were sleeping
escaped goblin and reached your kingdom,
arrived at hotel del luna smelling freedom.

Dived into Olive Young
travelled to Han (river) & Namsan,
having a black card holder
didn't worry converting INR & Won.

Got my reply in 1988
the future I never knew,
in love with the lead of every new drama
but home is 'in the soop' with you.

****

A Slice of Kimchi

A slice of kimchi in a bowl of rice
life is tastier with Korean spice.

A drink of soju and some sprite
life is hungover there's no respite.

A glass of champagne with some ice
life is tipsy hard but nice.

A squeeze of lemon on the salads
life is tangier with some lads.

A whiff of barbeque from the grills
life is living on the edge; seeking thrills.

A bite of pickle with biryani rice
life is scrumptious with hunky boys.

A sprinkle of salt on the sides
life is a surprise like a rolling dice.

A dash of fun in a platter of love
life is healthier seeing those eyes…

A bowl of ramen or coffee to go
life is merrier with someone besides.

A slice of kimchi on a plate of fries
life is calling me, to be a Korean's wife.

****

Heartthrob

I love you like crazy
don't ever set me free,
promise to never leave you alone
hope my dream becomes a reality.

If I ruled the world
and we meet face to face
ZM-illennial could be our escape place.

Address a letter, I'm 'parked' home
I'll not lie, to your tunes I'll vibe
take me wherever
Seoul or Busan I will roam.

With your moon tattoos
imaginations running wild,
forever young at heart
can't write in here, never mind.

Who's my muse?
an angel who always shines,
it'll feel like a rebirth
pick your filter
will you be mine?

****

Sonnet

Swollen up emotions pent up inside

when you came, happiest day of my life.

I had my doubts if ever I will have you,

it's a blessing from God, that you chose me

in all your steps I will be there with you.

First time you held my hand and didn't let go,

lost track of time, busy clicking photos.

I will endure your tantrums, make you smile,

you please take care of me once in a while.

I will read, sing, cook, care for you always,

don't be mad at me if I lose my cool,

love you unconditionally, that's my rule.

No one can break, even if on different sides,

a bond so strong, a mother and her child.

****

Rare

Another day, another night
countless stars under the limitless sky
as pure as petrichor
an intangible love that is infinite.

Deep waters of the ocean
endless sand in the desert
hot flames of fire
invisible air present everywhere,
five elements of nature
basic and not rare.

A rare comet
a rare pure blue diamond
a possibility to see these on earth, than
a newfound love that's unearthed.
A one-sided love affair
dangerously common and not rare.

Mysteries of the earth
unexplained but there,
unrequited love
beautiful and not unfair…

No regrets whatsoever
one day it might come true
when a turtle wins over a hare.

****

Frozen Winter

In a quaint village
under the moonlit sky,
a wooden cottage
and snowfall on the side.

Chilly winds on foggy nights
a fireplace
with views of the hill side,
a quilt, a hot cup of coffee
what's comfier,
a romantic lover who's a hottie.

Celebrating new years or valentines
covered in layers, hands intertwined
what's warmer
the closeness felt this time.

Welcome winters
in a picturesque place,
what's cooler
an amazing man
with more than just a pretty face.

****

Twisted

Is it
love fetched far?
met never,
it is mystery.
Love with boy
unknown, known.
Reason to smile
platonic and pure,
perfect is life?

Hmm...

Life is perfect
pure and platonic.
Smile to reasons
known, unknown.
Boy with love
mystery, is it?
Never met,
far-fetched love
it is.

****

Seasons

Winter, autumn
summer or spring
in all seasons
a globetrotter with wings.

The cloudy sky
the windy days
the setting sun
the rising waves,

The winter air
the summer haze
meeting eyes
hearts ablaze.

A hot cup of ramen
with chilled sprite,
no alarm clock days
and pleasant dreamy nights.

Slow mornings, lazy afternoons
breezy evenings and tranquil nights,
living in the moment
and enjoying the quiet…

Dry leaves of autumn
fresh flowers of spring
scorching summer heat
or winter frost on wings.

Slight drizzle or downpours
in all seasons
don't want to be lonely
just want to be yours.

Rain be pouring
sky keep falling
seasons change oh na, na, na
Don't wanna be fool, wanna be cool
wanna be loved; in the seasons that rule.

Don't tell me bye (bye)
you make me cry (cry)
each season
deeper, yeah, I think I'm going deeper,
love rising on high (high).

****

The Firmament

Wishing on a star
reflection so bright,
a seesaw of emotions
like lotte world rides.

Gazing from afar
pining for my star,
a whirlwind of emotions
like tidal waves are.

Dear my friend
with blueberry eyes
like moon at perigee
always shining bright.
Locked in a safety zone
in my heart, in my sight.

Hold my hands and talk endlessly
I know you miss me too
close your eyes
you know where to find me,
I know you love me
in my world all of this is true…

Is it only left for poetry
a star and its romance?
what's it like in your world
does a grain of sand stand a chance?
a star and its lover, do they meet
or is it forever a stealing glance?

****

Home

Visit another peninsula
my soulmate at Seoul,
please come someday
you're welcome to my home.

Trekking to the highest motorable road
or the grandeur of palaces to roam,
together in this journey
you're welcome to my home.

Sightseeing the highest statue
or visiting the wettest place on earth,
drenched from head to toe
you're welcome to my home.

Munching on the local cuisine
and sipping some chai
not a tourist, but you'll feel at home
this place is away, just a few thousand miles.

With your concerts
at largest stadium of the world
get your mind swirled
and at the largest center for meditation
experience tranquility & divine intervention…

Backpacking to the snow-clad Himalayas
or the mighty desert land
hill stations of Himachal, scenic beaches
or the coral reef Andaman Islands.

Together in this journey
from your home to mine
Namaste, please come someday
it will be divine.

Home is where you are
a fact that is known,
a place that borders east, south and yellow sea,
'You know I want that home
you know you got that home'.

****

Seashore

Walking barefoot on a beach
and you within my reach,
watching waves, holding hands
brushing our feet is soft sand.

Lying down facing the sky
counting the stars so high,
just stay here in my arms
don't say good bye.

A song in the background
with candle lit dinner ashore,
clinking glasses, close dances
love story furthermore.

What's more attractive
the wind ruffling your hair
or the love present in the air?

A date by the seashore
unable to overcome the whirlpool,
that song is so true
a special someone
melts my heart into two.

****

Villanelle

Dark clouds gathering the rain
respite from dry spell
it washes away all the pain.

Walking across Gangnam bylanes
pondering about life now & then
dark clouds gathering the rain.

Out of the mundane misery and now sane
a short spell of love shower
it washes away all the pain.

Soaked in all that came
hailstorms or heat waves or
dark clouds gathering the rain.

Blizzards, thunderstorms, hurricanes
come what may, love...
it washes away all the pain.

Seeking a mirage but in vain
drought all over, but all of a sudden
dark clouds gathering the rain
it washed away all the pain.

****

An Ode

All the rage around you
you were so popular,
when I first saw you
I was just a teenager.

You looked so fine
wanted you badly,
having a companion was a fad
many years after
my wish did become a reality.

Hooked onto for hours
time flew when I held you,
touched all the right keys
couldn't take my eyes off you.

Alas! this relationship didn't last forever
and all of a sudden, I lost you,
dejected and heartbroken
but I soon came over you.

Hitting the right curves
the touch so smooth,
smart and swanky
found someone new.

Watching movies, capturing good memories…

listening songs, listening to my stories.

Besides me whenever I need,
wakes me up, puts me to sleep.
Never out of style
with me at my lows & highs.

Keeps me entertained
always charged up,
no down time
sleek and covered up.

Stop acting pricey
I won't abandon you,
you know my secrets
hope I don't lose you.

Can't take you in the shower
rest all the times I'm with you,
on my pillow, on my table
my dear phone,
this is my ode to you.

It's always been you the goodlooking one
in a world of iPhones,
you're my one & only love, Samsung.

****

If

If I was a few years younger
or if you were older to me,
if we were of the same age
and born in the same country.

If we were classmates
and you had a crush on me,
if we were high school sweethearts
how cute that would be.

If we were neighbours
and you sneaked in to meet me,
if it was our first love
how perfect that would be.

If we were colleagues
and had an office romance,
if I was a celebrity
and you were my fan,
your fan letters
would make me your stan.

If we were strangers which we are
how would our little meet-cute be?
If we were lovers or best friends forever
how special that would be…

If we were married
how close would we be?
if we were soulmates
would love you unconditionally.

Even if all this is not true
would hold onto you till infinity,
I know you are super star
would orbit around you to eternity.

Wish I could turn back time,
only if and if only.

****

Ms. You

I think of you most of the time
wondering what it would be like,
my 'me' time is you
in you, my happiness resides.

I close my eyes when I miss you
and you're there every single time,
each day a different scenario playing
where Y/N is truly sublime.

On days I'm happy
on days I'm sad
wish I could share it with you
You, if I had.

On days I am sad
your words ring in my head,
everything will be ok
towards you my comfort heads.

Hear my voice through the silence
long distance isn't the roadblock,
in the midst of all the chaos
one thing is certain
around you my life revolves…

I wish all your wish come true
and you be happy with your soulmate,
on the other side of the world
there's someone who still awaits.

From a distance I'll continue loving you
knowing you're with someone else,
I'll support you in all the ways I can
in you my heart rests.

I want you to have the best of everything
you've given me the world and so much more,
the best thing that happened to me is you,
It is you that my heart adores.

****

Folklore

About 2000 years ago in the first century
there lived a princess in Ayodhya
that moved to another country.

The folklore of Ayodhya and Korea,
some believe & some don't in this theory.
Queen Heo Hwang-ok and King Kim Suro,
this is their story.

The heavenly gods appeared in her parent's dream
and told them to send their daughter
Suri Ratna to Suro,
He who had been chosen as Gaya's king,
King Kim Suro.

The king had not yet found a queen
and was waiting for a celestial sign
he did not marry the local maidens
as he knew it wasn't the right time.

The princess sailed
and reached the Gaya kingdom
knowing both their fates are intertwined.

She crossed the ocean covering 3000 miles
with her entourage she sailed for two months
till she reached the Korean skies…

She found Beondo,
a peach that was extremely rare
which fruited only once in 3000 years there.

To escort princess and her courtiers to the palace
the king sent his chiefs to the island,
the princess denied to accompany strangers
so, the king ordered to make a tent near the mainland.

She carried precious jewels, gems, gold, silver, silk,
offered them to mountain gods
before marrying the king.
People remember her to this day
marrying King Suro
Princess Suri Ratna became Queen Heo Hwang-ok.

She had 12 children with the king,
in present day
many believe to be direct descendants of her clan,
how divine is this love story
between two peninsular lands.

Legendary tale of these two royals
still relevant to this time
there exists a memorial in her name
in both the countries; yours and mine.

****

Haiku

Lonely but not lone
best things in life are for free
but there's someone.

It's true love wins all
music, songs, love, unites all.
Best thing summarized.

All inspirations
from a sole far source but near
thank you so much dear.

Haters gonna hate
we don't give a penny. We're,
Bulletproof family.

Just three words to sway
not 'I love you' but clearly
BTS paved the way!!

Spread the word in clan
get people go frenzy, it's
Bangtan Sonyeondan…

Tanka

A date with heartthrob
by seashore, a rare love dream.
Hope it is soon done,
proposal like song or ode
Best time spent is with 'the one'.

****

Songster

A connoisseur of music
with room full of artwork
articulate, strong built
bright and shiny like a flower, flower work.
Want to wrap you in my (a)rm
I love you and your musical work.

No one can match
to your worldwide handsomeness
when I'm with you there's no one else,
of super tunas I'm jealous
but I'll be there for you, oh, oh, oh
you are the reason for my happiness.

Who's the king, who's the boss?
the shy cat who loves tangerines,
my future's gonna be okay
on you I can lean.
A gummy smile and a juicy chat
now that, that I like that.

Every time I walk, every time I run
think of your song
let's burn, burn, arson.
Hope you don't judge me, Ddaeng!
popping, rocking, hopping, tutting, dougie, flexing,
swagging' WOO!!
I know nothing, can't I just dance with you?...

Angels don't fly so close to me
but yeah I got that vibe,
just in my imaginative nights
you spin me up high.
I can be your Jiminie
finally free from resentment
I love you babe is an understatement.

If there's winter ahead
I'll be with you all the time
wish we could slow dance till the spring comes by.
Just want to be where you are
don't put an end to this friendship of ours.

Standing next to Bam's dad
I'll be feeling the rush left and right,
take my hands now
I just want to see you like that.
If you want to come, come with me,
I'll be loving you right.

Yolo yolo ya, or everybody say la la la la la
is this your favourite song?
I may not understand Korean
but I know where my heart belongs…

They call me (call me)
Bitsy,
Hazy
is what they say,
but my calling; I'm chasing.

Thinking about you
rocking, rolling, swagging, swagger,
is it wrong?
forever and ever are we young?

Don't mind just one day
some day with you,
it's my inner narrator saying
I love you.

****

Under the Spell

As days goes by, at times I feel low
But seeing the finer things in life I feel blessed
'Coz, I need to stay positive and find a hobby
Do things that I like and not worry.
Even if it doesn't matter to anyone else
For my sanity, for myself.
Great to have a family to celebrate
Holidays with.
In life's daily hustle and bustle
Just want few days of relaxing the muscles.
Kind heartedness goes a long way
Living alone to this day.
May be in alternate reality
New beginnings will follow.
Oh, how much I am waiting
Pining for a lover and somehow feel hollow.
Quest for love is never ending
Road is long, need to cross one ocean and many seas.
Someday it might be possible
To believe what others say:
"Umm this is never going to happen"
Very least I can do, not let my spirits dampen.
When, where, how I don't know yet.
X's don't matter, for the future one I will strive
Yes, I will keep that hope and
Zeal in me alive.

****

Proposal

"Hey, how you doing?"
not like this...
"You want to eat ramen?
not like this either.

I know you
but I want to know you better
don't avoid this stranger
will you go out with me?
I'm new to your city.

I find you attractive
I find you cute
you're so lovable
than my eyes are seeing,
you're the one and only being.

Maybe we can go for a stroll
or watch a movie,
walk hand in hand
all lovey-dovey.

Dinner at your favourite place
or wherever you say,
I just want to watch your pretty face…

No need of bodyguard Lee
I'll take care of you from prying eyes,
I love you so much
just it’s me I'm nice.

About me?
I'm a simple girl next ~~door~~ country
no special talents just ordinary
what'll make it special, is your company
I'll wait for your reply,
meanwhile here's a ring from Tiffany.

****

Seven

Seven wonderful people
like the seven wonders of the world,
each with a unique persona
like the seven rainbow colours on earth.

The seven stars in the sky
angelic and beyond our reach
seven continents to explore
but one sole place, that's one in a crore.

Like the seven musical notes
one-of-a-kind & timeless,
seven singers
who are unparalleled and melodious.

Seven vows around the sacred fire
promises to last seven lifetimes,
a bond so perfect called marriage
in seventh heaven if one of them is mine.

Sacred is number seven
from the numbers that are infinite
a special place in our hearts
in the mysterious number game called life…

10 directions
9 planets
8 immortals
7 days of a week
6 strings of guitar
5 senses of the body
4 basic elements of life
3 essential qualities of nature
2 souls
1 life

****

Bangtan

A name so powerful - 'Bulletproof boy scouts'
princes of pop, there's no doubt.
Made a small company a big hit
millions of fans who love them to every bit.

Won largest number of awards
beating all-time records,
breaking the language barrier
made people dance, sing and happier.

Global icons whom world respects
not knowing them earlier, the only regret.
They are thorough gentlemen
who knows how to respect women.

A name so powerful
made lives wonderful.
Glamourous lifestyles but stay in fan's heart
rich but modest, made their nation proud.

A force to reckon with,
in love with them and their music.
2, 3, Bang, Bangtan
here to stay for decades with a bang!

****

Acrostic

Boys from another land rocking global music
As talented as one can be,
Never in my wildest dreams ever thought
Got learning a new foreign language simply.
To sing the lyrics correctly
And
Not just mumble anything incorrectly.

So far have just learned slang words
Oh, you think I am wild?
No, I'm meek but crazy once in a while.
Yet to follow my dreams
Eager to know what they are
Oh! coz, I don't know yet where they are.
Never hurts to remind oneself 'love yourself'
Do you feel overwhelmed with all the love?
Anybody else doesn't stand a chance,
Never will I back off till I have that first dance.

Because today's supreme
Because tonight's sweetest
together I love these letters B, T, S.

****

5 W, 1 H

Who is this person
making me weak in the knees,
the number '7' tattooed guy
keeping me awake in my sleep.

What to do next, I don't have it sorted
all I can do is not move on,
a corner of my heart
to you it always belongs.

Why are we away,
will time bring us together?
maybe need a magic spell
" Wanna money, money..."
that'll work faster.

Where are you?
in my fan letters, on my screen
in you tube, in insta reels.
You can find me
in birthday wishes, in voting polls
in comment sections of the posts.
Find me and I'm gonna live with you
find me and I'm gonna bleed with you
why, when, where, how? get the cue…

When we'll be together
you needn't worry,
together we'll take on this world
there's no hurry.

When you need me
I'll be there,
I'll save you from all the phonies.
But let's take the first step before the doom,

How do I say I love you
is it too soon?
waited a lifetime,
in my mind your answer looms.

****

How it Began

A random Instagram reel
popped up on my screen,
kept scrolling further
deeply intrigued.

As someone said
once you Jim in you can't Jim out,
now there's no looking back
seven precious people
are locked up in my heart.

All I wanted was
to know their names,
don't know how I fell in love
fascinated with their fame.

Was it their music
was it their funny, quirky style
was it their looks
or their down-to-earth side?

Was it their simplicity
was it their modesty
or was it their loving, charming side?...

It's all of the above, I guess
knowing them was the best time spent
my gratitude, my respect
love you my beloved BTS.

****

Bonus Verse

Guess the song

Do you feel my love
do you feel my love
I bet you there's not a better pick (better pick)
tell me where you at
tell me where you at
I'll come flying to you very quick. (very quick)

I'll follow you, follow you till my time's up
you're so tempting n tempting can't give up
can I latch onto you, will you hold up
may I dare, may I dare, may I dare?

A love story, you've found 'em
too many can you share 'em,
love drops, love drops,

La, la oh fish, fish, la la oh fish, fish

I can't stop me; I'm bound to crop up
too cheesy, you know I can't get enough
love drops, love drops,

My, my I wish, wish, my, my I wish, wish…

Baby, watch your surround (surround)
I'm nowhere to be found (found)
you stopped me from whine (whine)
and taught me to smile (smile)
look here in my heart, the same new me
you know how I feel, damn happy.

(Turn Up)

how many hours have I sighed,
I keep on dreaming on the cloud,
down in the ocean or up in the sky
everyday I'm waiting, for love drop's dam.

Do you feel my love....

Hopers gonna hope
lovers gonna love
you're my life man
wish me good luck!

****

Conclusion

Hope this book finds its reader
or the author finds its muse,
please meet me oh 7 good lookers
I'll let you win rock, paper, scissors
and also, the ramen cooker.

- A Book by Bhardwaj Tiwari Neha

Korean Name:
Kim Min Jeon Jung Park ARMY

****

this page is intentionally left blank
to scribble your thoughts or get autographs.